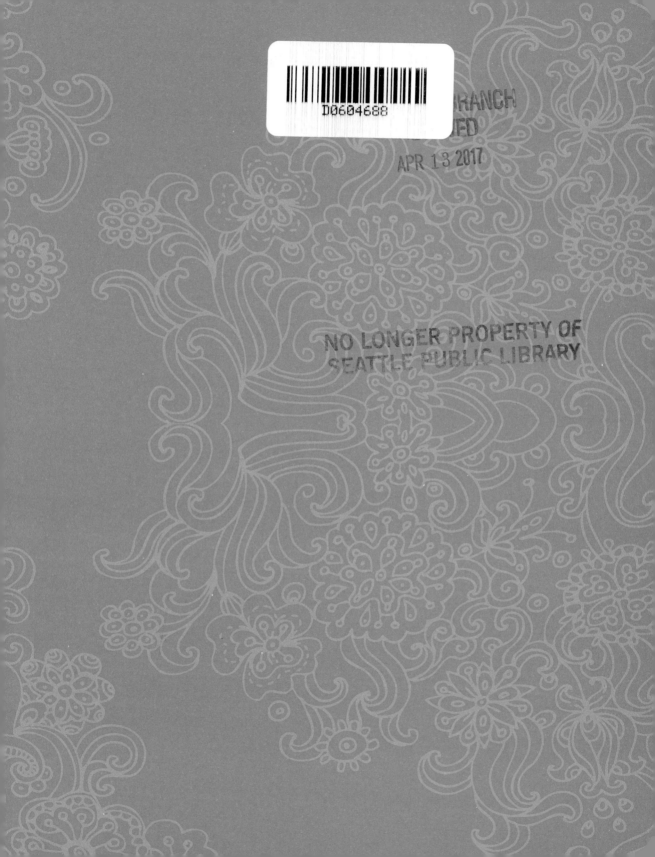

YOGA
FOR YOU

REBECCA RISSMAN

Walter Foster
Jr.

Quarto is the authority on a wide range of topics.

Quarto educates, entertains and enriches the lives of our readers—enthusiasts and lovers of hands-on living.

www.quartoknows.com

First published in the UK in 2016 by QED Publishing

Published in the USA in 2017 by Walter Foster Jr.,
an imprint of Quarto Publishing Group USA Inc.
All rights reserved. Walter Foster Jr. is trademarked.

6 Orchard Road, Suite 100
Lake Forest, CA 92630
quartoknows.com
Visit our blogs at quartoknows.com

Publisher: Maxime Boucknooghe
Art Director: Susi Martin
Editorial Director: Laura Knowles
Design: Clare Barber
Original illustrations: Colonel Moutard

The author and publisher would like to thank
Annie Pezalla for her invaluable help.

10 9 8 7 6 5 4 3 2 1

Printed in China

Contents

From Stressed to Serene

If you're feeling frazzled or frantic, a yoga class might be just what you need to relax. Yoga offers you a chance to slow down, settle down, and most importantly, calm down. An hour or so of deep breathing, stretching, and muscular exercise is just what you need to adjust your attitude. You'll leave class feeling like a new, happier you!

WHAT DO YOU NEED?

If you decide to catch a yoga class at a studio, you won't need to bring anything at all. Most studios allow students to borrow yoga props. These are tools that make a yoga practice easier or more comfortable. Yoga mats are the most common prop you'll see in a yoga studio. They help stop your feet and hands from slipping and provide a little cushioning. Other props include blocks or straps that can be used to make poses less challenging or intense.

WHEN THE WORLD GETS YOU DOWN...

YOGA STUDIO

FOOTWEAR

Take your trendy sneakers or fancy flip flops off at the door, please! Yoga is best done barefoot. Shoes can make it hard to balance in many different poses. They also interfere with the way different poses feel. If you're plagued by freezing feet, feel free to wear a pair of socks until your toes are toasty. Then take the socks off and enjoy the feel of your mat under your bare feet.

NO PROPS? NO PROBLEM!

Unlike other fitness activities, such as cycling or soccer, you don't need any special equipment to do yoga. In fact, the only thing you absolutely need to practice yoga is flat ground! This means there is absolutely no reason not to start adding a little yoga to your day.

DITCH YOUR STUFF

Most yoga studios will ask you to leave your belongings in a locker or shelf at the back of the room. Some will even require that your bags are placed outside of the studio. This might seem weird, but it's all part of your yoga practice. You can't do yoga if you're distracted by the buzzing of your cell phone from deep inside your bag.

...A LITTLE YOGA CAN TURN YOUR DAY AROUND!

What Is Yoga?

Have you ever overheard people talking about yoga? They may have used unfamiliar words such as "guru" or "asana." Or have you seen people walking around carrying rolled-up rubber mats? You might wonder what sort of mysterious activity involves a different language and bizarre props!

YOGA EVERYWHERE

Today, yoga is certainly a popular activity; more than 30 million people around the world now do yoga. People practice yoga in schools, churches, gyms, and yoga studios. Are you curious about what this activity is, and why so many people seem to love it?

Yoga is an activity that can help people improve their physical, mental, and emotional health. It helps people understand how their mental or emotional health affects their physical body, and vice versa. Practicing yoga involves working to unite the mind, body, and spirit, all of which are equally important to a person's well-being.

A brief history

Yoga was first practiced thousands of years ago in ancient India. It was part of a spiritual tradition that helped people find peace and self-awareness. Ancient yoga was mostly focused on meditation and controlled breathing.

Let's get physical

As time passed, yoga teachers, or gurus, began to focus more on the athletic component of yoga. They taught different poses, or asanas, in addition to breathing and meditation, and they started to travel outside of India to spread their philosophy and practice. In 1947, a yoga teacher named Indra Devi began teaching yoga to movie stars in Hollywood, California. Before long, yoga became a glamorous and popular way for people to get fit.

The word "yoga" comes from the Sanskrit word "yuj," which means to unite.

Why Practice Yoga?

Yoga is fun, relaxing, and has some amazing benefits for your mind, body, and spirit. You can practice yoga by yourself, or with your friends. You can even head to a yoga class to meet cool new people.

GOOD FOR YOUR BODY

Most people get into yoga for its physical benefits. Yoga is a safe way to build muscle, increase flexibility, and improve overall health.

Asanas challenge people to hold strenuous postures for several breaths. In a yoga practice, people often string together long sequences of asanas to work the muscles in the whole body.

The science of yoga

Researchers have discovered some amazing ways that yoga helps the body. They have learned that yoga can help people develop better breathing, balance, and posture.

Yoga often makes it easier for people to recover from injuries by reducing pain or helping to cope with discomfort. Doctors have even learned that yoga can improve the strength of people's bones!

Yoga benefits

Yoga is especially good for people who spend a lot of time sitting. It stretches and strengthens the muscles in the spine, legs, hips, and arms. These areas can grow stiff or tense after long periods of time in a chair or on a couch.

ISO-WHAT EXERCISE?!

Many yoga poses are isometric exercises. This means that they challenge a person to hold a muscle in a tensed position without moving. Pike Headstand Pose, for example, is a good isometric exercise. It involves keeping the abdomen, legs, arms, and back tensed for several breaths.

Yoga also boosts the body's immune system. This means that people who practice yoga are able to fight off many illnesses quickly and efficiently.

GOOD FOR YOUR MIND

Yoga is good for the mind as well as the body. Yoga helps people to relax and feel less stressed. It can boost people's moods and give them more energy. Yoga has even been shown to improve a person's ability to perform on academic tests! How can an hour-long activity do all of this? The secret is in yoga's three main elements.

YOGA IS MADE UP OF THREE PARTS:
* Physical poses
* Controlled breathing
* Meditation

OOOOOMMMMMMM
OOOOOMMMMMMM
OOOOOMMMMMM

Together, these three elements are great for the brain. Each yoga pose is made up of many different actions. Doing a pose correctly takes a lot of concentration. Juggling all the sensations of a difficult yoga pose, while also focusing on staying in the correct position, is an awesome exercise for the brain.

Time to de-stress

Yoga takes focus. Doing yoga makes people stop thinking about their worries in order to make sure they are doing the poses correctly. A yoga class often gives people a brief break from the things that cause them stress. Over time, it can really help a person's mood. People who practice yoga regularly report feeling happier and less worried.

Breathe in... and out

Have you ever told a worried friend to "take a deep breath?" Controlled breathing, called "pranayama," is a very important part of yoga. It involves taking long, deep breaths that are linked to different asanas. It sometimes involves holding the breath for a few seconds. This might sound simple, but it requires focus and self control. It is a great exercise to boost the brain's ability to concentrate.

MEDITATION MATTERS

Almost all types of yoga involve meditation. This is a quiet, focused practice that involves thinking about one thing—or nothing at all. Meditation can be difficult to get right, but it can improve heart health, reduce stress, improve sleep, boost energy, and even make people feel younger.

Some yoga teachers ask their students to sit in meditation for five or ten minutes at the beginning of class. Others simply provide a minute or two at the end of class for quiet reflection.

MINDFULNESS

A key component of yoga is learning to focus the mind, often referred to as mindfulness. Practicing mindfulness means thinking only of the things that are happening in the moment, rather than worrying about events in the future or in the past. Being mindful in yoga means thinking about your alignment in a yoga pose, the breath in your lungs, and the sensations you are feeling.

Scientists have discovered that meditating for even a very short amount of time can be beneficial for the brain.

GOOD FOR YOUR SPIRIT

Yoga isn't just good for your mind and body. It's also good for the part of you that can be hard to define: your spirit. When yoga teachers talk about the spirit, they are usually referring to a person's mood, emotional well-being, and sense of self.

Practicing yoga encourages people to focus on themselves. This can be hard for busy people who are used to focusing all of their energy on work, school, friends, or family. An hour-long yoga practice is a chance for people to take a break from their hectic lives and simply engage with their own body and mind.

"Ananda" is the Sanskrit word for bliss. In yoga, it is used to describe a feeling of utter freedom and happiness.

Adjust your mood

Focusing on the self helps people to become more aware of their mood. They might notice things that are bothering them, or stresses they were not aware of. Practicing yoga gives people a chance to work through emotional issues in a private, safe, and healthy way.

Feel the benefits

The physical and mental benefits of yoga often lead to spiritual benefits. After all, when someone is sleeping better, feeling fewer aches and pains, and doing better in school, it is easy to see how they might start to feel better about themselves! Yoga has even been scientifically proven to help improve people's moods.

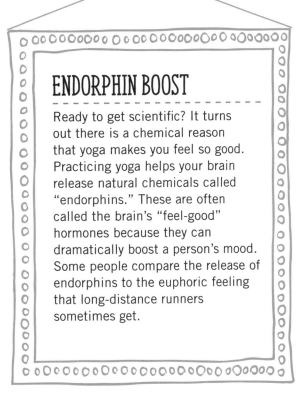

ENDORPHIN BOOST

Ready to get scientific? It turns out there is a chemical reason that yoga makes you feel so good. Practicing yoga helps your brain release natural chemicals called "endorphins." These are often called the brain's "feel-good" hormones because they can dramatically boost a person's mood. Some people compare the release of endorphins to the euphoric feeling that long-distance runners sometimes get.

IS YOGA A RELIGION?

Yoga teachers often instruct their students to bring their hands into "prayer position." This might make you wonder: Is yoga a religious activity? The answer is complicated. Yoga's historic roots come from religious traditions such as Hinduism and Buddhism. And some types of yoga encourage practitioners to follow a moral code and seek a higher power. However, most modern western yoga classes are very different from these historic types of practices.

Today, the vast majority of yoga that is practiced in western countries is not religious. People practice yoga in schools, businesses, and other public venues. People who do yoga in these classes understand that while some poses or sequences have religious-sounding names, such as Goddess Pose, they do not involve worshipping a higher power.

An Energizing Yoga Sequence

Ready to get pumped up and boost your energy?
Then roll out your yoga mat and let's get going!

An active yoga practice is a great way to improve your health, energy levels, and mood. To set up for a sweaty yoga session, kick off your shoes and put on some comfortable clothes. If you want to use a yoga mat or towel, roll it out on a flat area. If you enjoy listening to music, try to choose songs that won't distract you. Songs without words can be great for keeping you energized and focused.

Try this active yoga sequence the next time you're feeling sleepy or bored. Remember to do the asymmetrical poses twice—once on each side. If a pose feels really good or extra challenging, feel free to do it several times. After all, this practice is all yours!

DON'T PUSH IT

Never do a yoga pose that causes you pain! When done correctly, yoga poses might challenge your muscles or give you a deep stretch. They should never, ever hurt.

SANSKRIT NAMES

Many of these poses have names in Sanskrit as well as English. The Sanskrit names are provided underneath the English names. You can use whichever one you want, but you may hear the Sanskrit sometimes in a yoga studio.

Mountain Pose

Tadasana

Many yoga sequences begin with Mountain Pose. However, this posture is great to try on its own. It looks simple, but when practiced correctly, Mountain Pose works muscles all over your body.

1 Stand tall at the front of your mat with your big toes touching and your heels slightly apart.

2 Bring your hands to your sides, with your palms facing forward. Straighten your elbows and pull your shoulder blades closer to each other and down toward your bottom.

3 Relax your shoulders down, away from your ears.

4 Point your tailbone down toward your heels. Engage the muscles of your core by pulling your belly button in toward your spine.

5 Strengthen your legs by lifting your kneecaps up away from the floor.

6 Lift up through the crown of your head. Raise your chin slightly so that your jaw is parallel to the ground.

7 Hold for several long, deep breaths.

Standing Forward Fold Pose

Uttanasana

Standing Forward Fold Pose might look easy, but it can actually be quite challenging. In fact, the translation of the Sanskrit name for this pose means "intense stretch."

 From Mountain Pose, inhale deeply as you sweep your arms up toward the sky.

2 Exhale and bend at the hips to fold forward. Keep your hips directly over your heels.

3 Reach your arms down toward the floor. Rest your fingertips on your shins, ankles, or the floor outside your feet, depending on your flexibility.

If this pose feels too intense, bend your knees slightly. As you get more flexible, slowly work on straightening your legs more and more.

4 Relax your neck so that the crown of your head points down. If your neck feels tight, try gently nodding or shaking your head from side to side.

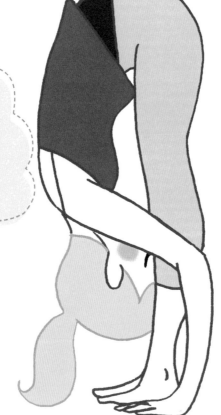

Half Forward Fold Pose

Ardha Uttanasana

Moving from Standing Forward Fold Pose into Half Forward Fold Pose can help you start to link your movement with your breath. Try to match the length of your inhale to your transition between these two poses.

Half Forward Fold Pose is a great stretch for your legs, but it's also a nice way to lengthen and strengthen your back. Try to focus on making your back as long and strong as you can.

1 From Standing Forward Fold Pose, inhale and lift the crown of your head and shoulders away from the floor.

2 Straighten your elbows and press your palms into your shins or ankles to elongate your back.

3 Pull your belly button in toward your spine.

4 Extend the crown of your head forward to make your back as straight as possible.

NEXT STAGE

If you were able to bring your palms to the floor in Standing Forward Fold Pose, then in this pose, try to press your fingertips to the floor and extend through the crown of your head.

Plank Pose

Plank Pose is a challenging asana that strengthens your arms, legs, and core. It can also give you a great mental workout.

1 From Half Forward Fold Pose, exhale and place your palms flat on the mat outside your feet. Your hands should be about shoulder-distance apart. Spread your fingers.

2 Step both feet to the back of your mat.

3 Rest your weight on the balls of your feet. Keep your heels lifted. Your feet should be about hip-distance apart.

4 Engage the muscles of your core to pull your belly button in toward your spine.

5 Straighten your back as much as possible. Try to make a straight line from your heels through the crown of your head.

6 Inhale and rock your weight slightly forward so that your shoulders are directly above your wrists.

CLEAR YOUR MIND

When you hold Plank Pose, you might find yourself thinking only about how hard it is. Instead of allowing your thoughts to focus on the challenge of the pose, try to think about taking long, smooth breaths.

High-to-Low Pushup
Chaturanga Dandasana

Chaturanga Dandasana is Sanskrit for "Four-Limbed Staff Pose." This name is a good reminder that each hand and foot plays an important role in supporting the body. Press into both hands and feet evenly while you work on this posture.

GETTING IT RIGHT

This movement is HARD! If it feels too challenging, bring your knees to the mat and try it again. It is much better to do this High-to-Low Pushup on your knees with the correct alignment in your arms and back than to do the full version with poor form. In fact, doing this movement incorrectly could hurt you!

1 Exhale and bend your elbows to slowly lower your body halfway down toward the mat. Keep your elbows hugging your sides. Do not let them bow out as if you were doing a traditional pushup.

2 When your elbows are bent at a right angle, stop.

3 Try to keep a straight line running from your heels through your hips and to the crown of your head. Let your gaze point down toward the mat.

Upward Facing Dog Pose
Urdhva Mukha Svasanana

Upward Facing Dog Pose is a great way to incorporate backbends into your yoga practice. It is typically only held for a breath, so enjoy that deep spinal stretch while it lasts!

If this pose feels too intense, try Cobra Pose. Bring your knees down to the mat and keep your elbows slightly bent. This will give you a gentler backbend but still work the same muscles as Upward Facing Dog Pose.

1 From High-to-Low Pushup, point your toes and shift your weight onto the tops of your feet. Inhale and straighten your arms.

2 Drop your hips toward the mat until your body comes into a backbend.

3 Flex the muscles in your legs so that your knees lift away from the mat.

4 Press your shoulders down away from your ears and lift the crown of your head up. Keep your gaze forward.

5 Flatten your palms onto the mat. Press especially into the thumb and forefinger of each hand.

Downward Facing Dog Pose
Adho Mukha Svanasana

Downward Facing Dog Pose stretches the muscles in your legs, hips, and shoulders. It is also a good strengthening exercise for your core and arms.

1 From Upward Facing Dog Pose, exhale and flip your feet one at a time to rest your weight on the balls of your feet.

2 Use the muscles in your core to lift your hips up toward the ceiling. Your body will form an upside-down V shape.

3 Press your heels down toward the mat and straighten your knees as much as you can.

If this feels too intense for you, bend your knees slightly. Hold this pose for a few breaths, and then take a break by dropping your knees to the ground. Then try it again. Before long, you'll be able to hold it for longer periods of time.

4 Press all parts of your hands into the mat, and try to make a straight line from your wrists up through your hips.

5 Pull your belly button in toward your spine.

6 Stay in Downward Facing Dog Pose for several breaths.

High Lunge Pose

Moving from Downward Facing Dog Pose into standing poses is an excellent way to work your core, leg, arm, and upper back muscles.

1 From Downward Facing Dog Pose, inhale and lift your right leg high into the air behind you. Extend through your heel and press your hands firmly into the ground. Try to make a long, straight line from your heel to your wrists.

2 Using your core muscles as much as possible, exhale and step your right foot in between your hands.

Don't worry if your foot doesn't make it all the way between your hands in one try! Be patient and take as many steps as you need.

3 Keep your left leg straight and your left heel lifted away from the mat. As you inhale, lift your hands from the floor onto your right knee.

5 Inhale and lift both arms straight up. Face your palms toward one another. Keeping your left leg very straight, aim both sides of your hips toward the front of the mat.

4 Exhale and press your hands down into your knee to straighten your back as much as you can.

6 Hold for several long, deep breaths.

Warrior Two Pose

Virabhadrasana II

Moving from High Lunge Pose into Warrior Two Pose is an intense stretch on your hips, ankles, and feet. It is also a great strength builder for your legs, back, and arms.

1 From High Lunge Pose, keep your right leg still as you turn your left heel down to the mat. Rotate your hips and shoulders to face the left side of your yoga mat.

2 Stretch your arms out to the sides. Turn your palms down toward the floor.

3 Inhale and straighten your back as much as you can by lifting the crown of your head toward the ceiling. Make sure your shoulders are over your hips, and that you aren't leaning toward the front of your mat.

4 Exhale and press your right big toe into your yoga mat. This will help your right knee stay directly above your right ankle.

5 Inhale and press the outer edge of your left foot into the yoga mat while focusing on keeping your left leg very straight.

6 Exhale and look out over your right hand. Lift your chin slightly to keep your neck long.

7 Hold for several long, deep breaths.

This pose can be very challenging on your muscles. If you need a break, straighten your right knee for a breath or two, then return to the pose.

Extended Side Angle Pose

Utthita Parsvakonasana

This lunging posture works the muscles in your legs while twisting your core and stretching the muscles in your shoulders.

1 From Warrior Two Pose, inhale and lift the crown of your head slightly to elongate your back.

2 Exhale and bring your right forearm down to the top of your right thigh. Your right palm should face up.

3 Extend your left arm over your head with your palm facing down. Straighten your left elbow to make a straight line from your left ankle through your left fingertips.

4 Inhale and open your chest to the left. Try to bring your left shoulder above your right shoulder.

5 Keep your left leg very straight. Press into the outer edge of your left foot.

6 Keeping your neck in line with the rest of your spine, look up toward the ceiling.

7 Hold this pose for a few deep breaths.

HEALTHY KNEES

To keep your knees safe, always remember these rules:

• Bend your knee at a 90-degree angle directly above your ankle. An over-bent knee will hover in front of the ankle, over the toes. This can cause knee stress or even injury.

• Don't allow your knee to splay out to the side. Press into the inner ball of your foot to keep your knee in correct alignment.

• If it hurts, stop! Never do a pose that causes you pain in your knees.

Warrior Three Pose

Virabhadrasana III

Warrior Three Pose can be a tricky balance. If you are having trouble holding this pose, try to focus your gaze on something still that is just in front of your yoga mat on the floor.

1 From Extended Side Angle Pose, exhale and look down at your front foot. Turn your top shoulder down to square your torso toward the front of your mat. Pivot your back foot to lift the heel away from the mat.

2 Inhale and bring your hands to your hips.

3 Exhale and lift your back foot off the mat as you straighten your front leg. Keeping your hands on your hips, lower your upper body so that it is parallel to the floor. Your body will form the shape of a capital T.

4 Straighten your lifted leg and press through the heel to bring it in line with your upper body. Point your heel up toward the ceiling.

5 Inhale and slowly extend your arms forward with the palms facing in. Try to keep your arms in line with your upper body and lifted leg, all forming a straight line that is parallel to the floor.

6 Hold this pose for a few deep breaths, then do the pose on the opposite leg.

Side Plank Pose
Vashistasana

Side Plank Pose can be a very difficult posture. It challenges you to balance on just one hand and one foot.

One of the most challenging things about Side Plank Pose is keeping your hips from sagging toward the floor. To prevent this, try to lift them even higher than you think they need to be.

1 From Warrior Three Pose, exhale and bring both hands down to the mat. Step both feet to the back of your mat to come into Plank Pose.

2 Inhale and roll onto the outer edge of your right foot. Stack your left foot directly on top of your right, or if that is too challenging, step it behind your right foot or knee to provide a little extra support.

3 Extend your left arm straight up with your palm facing forward. Try to make a straight line from your top wrist down to your bottom wrist.

4 Lift your chin away from your chest so that you can extend through the crown of your head.

5 Hold this pose for a few breaths.

Revolved Lunge Pose

Revolved Lunge Pose is an amazing pose on its own, but it is also a great jumping off point for other fun yoga poses. When you work on this pose, feel free to explore other movements that might feel good.

GET CREATIVE!

When you work on this pose, think creatively about how you might modify it for your body. If you want more of a twist, try straightening both arms, bringing your bottom hand just outside your bottom foot, and your top arm straight up. If you want a gentler pose, bring your back knee down to the ground.

1 From Side Plank Pose, exhale and return to Downward Facing Dog Pose.

2 Inhale and step your left foot forward, between your palms.

3 Exhale and keep your right heel lifted and your right leg straight.

4 Inhale to lift your hands away from the mat. Bring both palms together at the center of your chest.

5 Exhale deeply and bring your right elbow to the outside of your left knee. Press your palms into one another.

6 Extend through the crown of your head. Shift your gaze over your left elbow.

7 Hold for several breaths.

Bound Locust Pose

Salabhasana

Bound Locust Pose strengthens the back while stretching the muscles of the core.

If interlacing your fingers behind your back is too intense, hold onto a towel or belt with both hands instead.

1 From Revolved Lunge Pose, bring both hands down to your yoga mat. Step both feet to the back of your mat to come into Plank Pose. Exhale and lower to your belly. Rest your legs, arms, and forehead down onto the mat.

2 Point your toes and bring your big toes to touch.

3 Interlace your hands behind your lower back.

4 Inhale and press your knuckles toward your heels as you lift your upper body away from the floor. Keep your gaze down toward the floor and extend through the crown of your head.

5 Exhale and lift your heels away from the floor while keeping your legs very straight.

6 Hold for a few breaths, then lower back onto the floor.

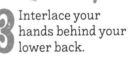

Bow Pose

Dhanurasana

This pose is named after the shape of an archer's bow. Can you see why?

1 From your position on your belly, bend your knees until your feet are close enough to your bottom for you to grab the outer edges of each ankle.

2 Inhale and begin to slowly pull your ankles away from your bottom. This will start to pull your shoulders up and off of the mat. Keep your gaze focused just in front of you.

3 Exhale and continue to pull your ankles away from your bottom. If this feels challenging enough, stay here. If you want more of a stretch, start to lift your knees away from the mat.

4 Hold for a few breaths and then lower back down to your belly.

If you can't reach your ankles, don't worry! Just hold on to a belt, towel, or yoga strap and loop it over your ankles.

Hero Pose
Virasana

Sitting in Hero Pose is a great way to catch your breath and find your focus.

1 From Bow Pose, exhale and release your grip on your ankles. Straighten your legs as you lie down on your belly.

2 Press onto your hands and knees as you inhale. Bring your knees closer together and slightly separate your heels. Point your toes.

3 Exhale and sit your bottom between your heels. If this is too deep of a stretch on your knees, place a block or folded blanket under your bottom.

4 Bring your hands onto your thighs, palms facing up. Bring your index fingers and thumbs together.

5 Lift up through the crown of your head to sit very tall. Drop your shoulders down, away from your ears. Pull your belly button in toward your spine.

6 Slightly lift your chin so that your lower jaw is parallel to the floor. Close your eyes.

7 Hold this pose for several breaths.

Child's Pose

Balasana

Child's Pose offers a nice break from a challenging yoga sequence. Feel free to take a rest in Child's Pose at any point during your yoga practice.

FEELING BETTER?

After doing this vigorous yoga sequence, you probably feel rejuvenated, energized, and perhaps a little sweaty. Drink plenty of water and remember how easy it was to turn your day around with a little yoga!

1 From Hero Pose, return to your hands and knees. Separate your knees so that they are almost as wide as the mat, and bring your big toes to touch.

2 Exhale as you sink your hips back and bring your bottom down on top of your heels.

3 Rest your forehead down onto the mat and allow your outstretched arms to relax. Let your elbows rest on the mat.

Turn to page 50 to learn an extra pose, which is used to end many yoga sequences.

4 Close your eyes and breathe deeply for several breaths.

A Calming Yoga Sequence

Feeling stressed? Overwhelmed? Is your homework piling up? Take a deep breath. It's time to unwind with some relaxing yoga that will restore your sense of calm.

Practicing yoga is a healthy way to cope with stress and anxiety. Relaxing yoga sequences are often less physically challenging than other more vigorous practices. They include many seated, reclined, and forward folding postures. These types of poses can help you release tension and feel more at ease.

To set up for your relaxing practice, get comfortable. Change out of any restricting clothing and put on something soft and stretchy. If your hair is in a ponytail, try letting it down. Take off anything that might distract you, such as clinking jewelry. If you wear glasses, you might even enjoy taking them off for your practice.

Try this sequence the next time you need to de-stress. If a posture feels particularly good to you, stay in it for as long as you like. You might even try practicing some of these poses with your eyes closed, to stay focused on being relaxed.

When you work through this sequence, remember that you need to do the asymmetrical poses twice-once on each side.

SET THE SCENE

It's hard to relax if you're distracted. Before you begin a calming yoga practice, put away your schoolbooks, shut your door, and turn off your cell phone. Dim the lights and play some soothing music.

Reclined Cobbler's Pose
Supta Baddha Konasana

This relaxing posture is a great way to open your hips while relaxing your shoulders, neck, arms, and core.

1 Lie on your back with your arms extended down by your sides. Allow your palms to face up.

2 Bend your knees to slide your heels in toward your bottom. Bring the soles of your feet together and let your knees fall open to the sides.

3 Relax the muscles in your lower back. If this area feels tight, rock your hips very gently from side to side to release tension.

4 One at a time, press your shoulders away from your ears.

5 Close your eyes and relax the muscles in your face, belly, back, and legs.

6 Breathe deeply.

If this pose is too intense of a stretch in your hips and groin, slide your heels farther away from your bottom. If you need a deeper stretch, bring your heels in closer to your bottom.

Head-to-Knee Forward Bend
Janu Sirsasana

This asymmetrical forward bend is a great way to stretch the legs, back, hips, and shoulders.

KNEE SAFETY

If your bent knee doesn't rest comfortably on the mat, slide the sole of your right foot down to the inner left knee or calf. This will help your bent knee rest more easily.

1 After Reclined Cobbler's Pose, roll onto one side. Use your hands to press yourself up into a seated position.

2 Extend your left leg straight out in front of you. Straighten your leg as much as you can, and press your heel down into the mat. Your left toes and kneecap should point straight up.

3 Bring the sole of your right foot into your inner left thigh. Let your right knee fall down toward the floor.

4 Inhale and reach both arms over your head as you sit up as tall as possible. Extend the crown of your head up toward the ceiling.

5 Exhale and fold forward over your extended left leg. Loop a yoga strap around the sole of your left foot. Fold forward and hold onto the strap with both hands.

6 Breathe deeply and press the crown of your head toward the top of your left foot.

NEXT STAGE

If you want to try a more advanced version, don't use a strap. Instead, reach your hands for the outer edges of your calf, ankle, or foot. Some people can even interlace their fingers around the sole of their foot.

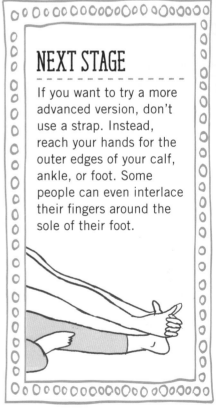

Reverse Tabletop Pose

If you spend a lot of time sitting at school or in front of a computer, you probably often allow your shoulders to slump forward. Reverse Tabletop Pose reverses this by stretching the shoulders, chest, and neck.

1 Sit on your bottom with your legs outstretched in front of you.

2 Lean back and place your hands about 6 inches (15 cm) behind your bottom. They should be shoulder-distance apart, with your fingers pointing toward your heels.

If dropping your head back in this posture feels like too much of a stretch in your neck, lift your chin so that your neck is parallel with the rest of your spine. Direct your gaze up at the ceiling.

3 One leg at a time, bend your knees and step your feet onto the mat. Try to have your feet directly under your knees.

4 Inhale and press into your hands and feet to lift your hips up. Ideally, your hips will be at the same height as your shoulders and knees.

5 Exhale as you allow your head to fall back. Close your eyes and relax.

6 Hold for a few breaths.

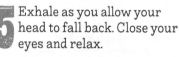

Reclining Revolved Eagle Pose

Supta Parivrtta Garudasana

Doing twisting poses in yoga can help you feel rejuvenated and invigorated. If you are hoping to keep calm and relaxed, do your twists on your back so that you don't get too energized.

1 Lie on your back with your arms and legs outstretched.

2 Bend your knees and lift both feet up off of the mat. Cross your left knee over your right.

3 Press your right foot into the mat to help you slide your hips over to the left about 1 inch (2.5 cm).

4 Exhale and allow both knees to drop over to the right.

If it's possible, wrap your left toes behind your right calf. If this is too intense, don't worry about it.

5 Inhale and extend both arms out to your sides in a T position with your palms facing up.

6 Try to keep both of your shoulder blades down on the mat.

7 Close your eyes and hold for a few breaths. If it feels good on your neck, drop your head to the left.

Supported Bridge Pose

Bridge Pose can be done with or without the support of your forearms. Using your forearms to help lift your hips can help you focus on staying calm rather than thinking about the challenge of holding this pose without support.

1 Lie on your back with your arms and legs outstretched.

2 Bend your knees and step your feet into the mat just in front of your bottom.

3 Extend your arms down at your sides and reach your fingertips toward your heels.

4 Exhale and press your hips into the air. Try not to allow your knees to fall open to the sides.

Have your feet about 6 inches (15 cm) apart, with your toes pointing straight ahead.

5 Inhale and bend your elbows. Bring your hands to your lower back with your fingertips wrapping around your hips. Rocking very gently from side to side, inch your elbows closer together until they are directly under your hips.

6 Exhale and relax the weight of your hips into your hands.

7 Look straight up and lift your chin away from your chest.

8 Hold for a few breaths.

Chair Pose

Utkatasana

Chair Pose is a great way to work your legs, core, and arms. It also stretches the muscles in your feet and shoulders.

1 Stand at the top of your mat with your big toes touching and your heels slightly separated.

2 Inhale as you bend your knees and lower your bottom as if to sit in a chair. At the same time, lift your arms straight up with your palms facing in.

3 Exhale as you pull your shoulder blades down your back and rock your weight into your heels.

4 Pull your belly button in toward your spine and look straight ahead.

5 Hold for several breaths.

WHAT'S IN A NAME?

You can probably see how Chair Pose got its name. When doing this posture, you lower your bottom down toward the ground as if you were going to sit on a chair. However, this pose also has another name: Lightning Bolt Pose. It's called this for two reasons: first, because the body makes the jagged shape of a lightning bolt, and second, because the pose is so energetic that some people say they feel electrified when they do it!

Side Bending Mountain Pose

This pose makes use of a mudra, a symbolic hand gesture used in yoga. The mudra is thought to have an effect on the flow of energy in the body and is used to complete a pose.

Parsva Tadasana

1 Stand at the top of your mat with your big toes touching and your heels slightly separated.

2 Inhale and lift both arms up. Interlace all of your fingers except your thumbs and index fingers.

3 Exhale and tip your fingers over to the right. Focus on pressing down through both legs evenly so that your hips don't sway to the left.

4 Inhale and extend through the crown of your head to lengthen your back.

SWITCH IT UP

Quick—interlace your hands in front of you. Now look: which thumb is on top? You probably interlace your fingers the same way every time you do this. In yoga, it's important to regularly switch the way you interlace your fingers. It might seem like a small detail, but over time, always interlacing your fingers in the same way can lead to one shoulder being more flexible than the other. This can cause problems in other poses.

5 Exhale and bend even farther over to the right. Try to keep your hips and shoulders in the same line. In other words, do not let your upper body bend forward.

6 Inhale and return to the center. Interlace your fingers with the opposite finger on top and repeat this pose, tipping to the left.

Ragdoll Pose

This is called Ragdoll Pose for a reason: when you're doing it, you let your upper body go limp, just like a ragdoll.

1 Stand at the top of your mat with your feet about 6 inches (15 cm) apart.

2 Put a deep bend in your knees and exhale as you fold forward.

3 Inhale to bring your hands to your opposite elbows. Let your head hang down toward the floor.

4 Very slowly, start to straighten your legs a little. Don't straighten them all the way.

5 Exhale to relax your upper body as much as possible. If you feel any tension in this pose, try gently nodding your head or rocking your upper body from side to side.

Even if you can straighten your legs in this pose, don't. Keeping a slight bend in your knees will help you get a nice stretch in your lower back.

Garland Pose

Malasana

Garland Pose is a deep stretch for the hips, calves, and feet. Try spending time in Garland Pose the next time you are watching TV.

1 From Ragdoll Pose, bring your fingertips to the floor and separate your feet a few inches farther apart. Point your toes slightly out to the sides and bring your heels closer together.

2 Exhale and drop your hips to come into a squatting position. Your heels might lift off of the mat when you do this. If it feels too intense, try rolling up a towel and placing it under your heels or simply separating your feet farther apart.

3 Inhale and bring your palms to touch in front of your heart. Press your elbows into your inner knees and press your knees back into your elbows.

4 Exhale and pull your belly in toward your spine.

5 Inhale and extend through the crown of your head as you straighten your back as much as you can.

GET ANOTHER VIEW

When done correctly, this is what Garland Pose will look like from the side.

Twisted Horse Pose

Parivrtta Utkata Konasana

Twisted Horse Pose might look a little complicated, but it's actually very simple. Try this pose the next time you feel tension in your back or hips.

1 Take a wide stance facing the side of your mat. Your feet should be about 3 feet (91 cm) apart. Turn your toes out and your heels in.

2 Exhale and bend your knees deeply to come into a wide squatting position. Bring your hands to your knees.

3 Inhale and keep your hips low as you lift through the crown of your head to straighten your back as much as possible.

4 Exhale and bring your right shoulder down toward the mat and lift your left shoulder up toward the ceiling. As you do this, your torso will lower down toward the floor.

5 Look over your left shoulder. Press your hands gently into each knee to deepen this spinal twist.

6 Hold for a few breaths and then repeat in the other direction.

Bound Wide Legged Forward Fold
Prasarita Padottanasana C

This forward fold gives you a great chance to stretch your legs and shoulders while also relaxing the muscles of your neck.

1 From Twisted Horse Pose, inhale and straighten your legs. Turn your toes in so that the outer edges of your feet are parallel. Bring your upper body upright.

2 Exhale and interlace your hands behind your lower back.

3 Inhale and straighten your elbows as much as you can.

4 Exhale and hinge at the hips to fold forward. Allow your hands to fall away from your bottom and up toward the ceiling. If you are very flexible, your hands might start to reach toward the floor.

If this is too deep of a stretch for you, hold onto a towel or yoga strap with both hands behind your back.

5 Relax the crown of your head down toward the floor. Push your shoulders toward your hips to keep your neck long and relaxed.

6 Press into all parts of your feet and lift your kneecaps up toward your hips.

7 Hold for a few breaths, then stand all the way back up.

Downward Facing Frog Pose
Adho Mukha Mandukasana

When viewed from above, your body
will look like a frog in this pose!

1 From Bound Wide Legged Forward Fold, bend your knees and bring both hands onto the mat.

2 Carefully come down onto the inner edge of each knee. Try to have your shins parallel to one another, and point your toes out to the sides. The inner edges of your feet will press down into the mat.

3 Exhale and bring your forearms down onto the mat.

4 Inhale and pull your belly button in toward your spine. Point your tailbone down to slightly round your lower back.

5 Exhale and very slowly move your hips back toward your heels until you feel a stretch in your groin. You might only shift your hips an inch or so.

6 Hold for a few breaths.

7 Inhale and rock your weight forward to come out of this pose.

Wide Angle Seated Forward Fold

Upavistha Konasana

Wide Angle Seated Forward Fold looks like an effortless pose, but it's not. Remember to keep your leg muscles engaged while you work on this deep stretch.

1 Sit on your bottom with your legs outstretched.

2 Spread your legs in a wide straddle. Keep your feet flexed with your toes and kneecaps pointing up.

3 Inhale and reach both arms straight up toward the ceiling. Make your back as straight and tall as you can.

4 Exhale and slowly fold forward. Allow your elbows to bend as you bring your hands to the mat in front of you. Your hands might rest just in front of your hips, or if you are more flexible, you might bring them farther out in front of you.

5 Keep extending through the crown of your head. Look straight ahead.

6 Hold for several breaths.

HOW WIDE?

It doesn't matter how wide you spread your legs in this pose. Whether you have your feet only as wide as your mat or in a full split, you will still get the benefits of this stretch. Just listen to your body and separate your legs wide enough for you to feel a deep stretch, but not so wide that you feel pain.

Gate Pose

Parighasana

This balancing posture can help you strengthen your legs and feet while you enjoy a deep stretch in your back and shoulders.

MOVE WITH IT

Gate Pose can be still or it can be full of movement. Try following your breaths to alternate between step 4 and step 5.

1 Start Gate Pose on your hands and knees.

2 Inhale and press into your legs to lift your upper body to an upright position.

3 Exhale and extend your right leg out to the right and straighten the knee. Press your right toes toward the floor. Press into the top of your left foot to help keep your balance.

4 Inhale and reach both arms straight up into the air.

5 Exhale and bring your right fingertips down to your right knee, shin, or ankle as you reach your left arm up and over your head. Don't put very much weight into your right hand. Use the muscles of your core to support your upper body as much as you can.

6 Gaze up under your left arm.

7 Hold for several breaths.

Forward Fold Pose
Paschimottanasana

Forward Fold Pose has many benefits. It can help you stretch your legs, back, and arms. Holding Forward Fold Pose with your eyes closed can also help relieve stress.

1 From Gate Pose, find a seated position on the mat. Extend both legs in front of you.

2 Bring your legs together and flex your feet. Engage the muscles of your legs by pulling your kneecaps up toward your hips.

3 Inhale and reach both arms up toward the ceiling. Grow as tall in your back as you can by extending the crown of the head up.

4 Exhale and reach both hands toward the outer edges of your shins, ankles, or feet. If this is too intense for you, put a slight bend in your knees.

5 Try to point the crown of your head at the tops of your feet.

6 Hold for several deep breaths.

WANT MORE?

If this pose doesn't feel challenging enough for you, deepen the stretch by changing the grip you have on your feet. Try interlacing your fingers around the bottoms of your feet. If you still want more, bend your elbows down toward the floor.

Happy Baby Pose
Ananda Balasana

It's not hard to guess where this pose got its name. Babies happily play with their feet like this all the time. When you try Happy Baby Pose, channel your inner baby and have fun with it!

1 From a seated position, slowly lower yourself all the way onto your back. Use your hands to pull your knees into your chest to form a ball.

2 Separate your knees wider than your ribs and lift your feet up toward the ceiling. Use your hands to grasp the outer edges of your feet. Allow your head to rest on the mat.

3 Exhale and gently pull your feet straight down toward the mat. This will bring your knees down toward the ground.

4 Either hold still, or rock from side to side to massage your hips and lower back.

5 Close your eyes and breathe deeply.

Reclined Pigeon Pose

Supta Kapotasana

This pose feels especially good after spending a long time in a seated position. Try it when you get home from school and enjoy the deep hip stretch.

1 From Happy Baby Pose, bring both feet onto the mat a few inches in front of your bottom with your knees lifted.

2 Lift your right leg to cross your right ankle over your left knee.

3 Inhale to reach your hands under your right shin and around either the left thigh or left shin. Interlace your fingers.

4 Exhale as you flex your left foot and gently use your hands to pull your left leg toward you.

5 Keep your neck relaxed and press both shoulders down into the mat. Gently press your right knee away from you.

The Final Pose: Corpse Pose

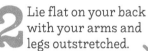

Savasana, or Corpse Pose, is often the last pose in a yoga practice. It can last for a few minutes, or half an hour or longer. Make sure you're comfortable before you do this pose.

If you feel any tension or discomfort in your lower back in this pose, roll up a towel and place it under your knees.

1 Get settled. If you are wearing shorts or a tank top, you might want to put on a sweater or pants. Remove glasses, hair ties, or any other items that may feel distracting.

2 Lie flat on your back with your arms and legs outstretched.

3 Separate your feet so they are about as wide as your mat. Let your feet fall open to the sides.

4 Move your hands a few inches away from your body. Face your palms up and allow your fingers to curl slightly in.

5 Rock your head from side to side to release any tension in your neck and shoulders. Then move your shoulders down away from your ears to lengthen your neck.

6 Close your eyes.

7 Relax the muscles in your whole body. Focus especially on releasing tension from your jaw, back, arms, and legs.

8 Try to allow your mind to become empty. If this is challenging for you, think about a single, peaceful image, such as a burning candle. Try not to become distracted by thoughts of school, friends, family, or anything else.

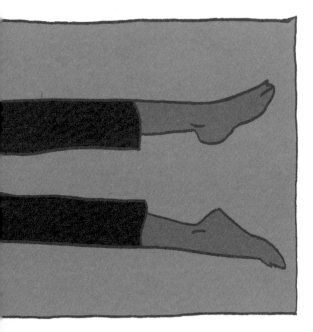

DID YOU SAY CORPSE?!

Sava is the Sanskrit word for "corpse," but the name is symbolic. In this pose, yoga students become as still and quiet as a corpse. When savasana is finished, they return to life with new energy and awareness.

If you are having a tough time staying focused during Corpse Pose, you're not alone. Ignoring distractions in yoga is hard, especially in a pose that is so easy to hold. Many people place a towel or eye pillow over their eyes during this pose to remind them to keep their eyes closed.

Choosing a Yoga Class

Now that you've had a chance to try out some yoga poses, you may want to start going to a weekly class. There are many different types of yoga, but whatever you're looking for, there is a class for you.

WHAT DO YOU WANT?

Think about what you want to get out of yoga. Do you want to practice yoga with a friend or by yourself? Are you looking for a relaxing practice, or do you want to really challenge yourself? Do you want to sweat, or are you hoping to go straight from yoga to your band practice without first sneaking in a shower?

Although countless unique styles of yoga exist, it's helpful to understand a few major types. The practices found within these branches of yoga typically share the same characteristics.

YOGA AT HOME

So you think you have to go to a gym or yoga studio to learn to practice? Think again! Yoga is an activity that can very easily be practiced alone at home. If you're new to yoga and need extra instruction, try visiting different yoga websites, listening to a yoga podcast, downloading an app on your phone, or following along with a DVD. When you get more experienced, you can move creatively through your own practice, focusing on whatever poses feel best to you.

Can't decide?

How are you feeling? Finding the right yoga class for you can depend a lot on your mood. Do you feel anxious or stressed? A relaxing Yin class might be the best fit for the day. Are you feeling energetic and ready for a challenge? Then you might want to try an Ashtanga class. The type of practice you choose today does not have to be the same as the practice you choose tomorrow. Listen to your mind and body, and choose the type with an activity level that seems like it will feel the best.

If you go to a gym or yoga studio, remember that each class will be a little different, depending on the teacher, location, and class size. If you don't like one class, don't get discouraged. Just try another one!

YOGA DISCIPLINES

Here are a few types of yoga you might encounter in yoga studios or gyms.

Acro Yoga

Looking for a thrill? Acro yoga might be the class for you. This modern style of yoga mixes yoga and acrobatics. To achieve some of the more amazing postures, acro yoga is typically practiced in pairs. If you decide to try this style of yoga, make sure to do so under the supervision of a trained instructor.

Hot Yoga

There are many different types of hot yoga. Some, such as Bikram yoga, are practiced in rooms that are as hot as 100-105 degrees Fahrenheit (38-41 degrees Celsius)! Other types use less extreme heat. The purpose of the heat is to help people stretch their muscles, sweat, and raise their heart rates. Practicing in the heat can be a healthy way to challenge your body, but remember to drink plenty of water. If you feel that you are becoming over-tired, sit down and take a break.

RESTORATIVE YOGA

Many different styles of yoga can be restorative. This means that it aims to relax the mind and body. Restorative yoga encourages people to hold different passive postures for several minutes at a time, often seated or lying down. The poses are easy for the muscles, focusing instead on stretching and relaxation. The slow, gentle, and calming pace of restorative yoga can help relieve anxiety, soothe aches and pains, and even help people get better sleep at night.

Vinyasa

Vinyasa yoga is an active, often very athletic type of yoga. This practice usually involves long sequences of challenging poses. Some vinyasa classes are called "flow" practices. This is because people flow, or move smoothly, from one pose to the next.

Ashtanga

Ashtanga is a challenging and advanced style of yoga. It involves different series of poses—each with a defined order—that are practiced over and over. Ashtanga is fast-paced and athletic. The classes often take place in a slightly warm room.

Yin

Yin yoga is quiet, slow-moving, and relaxing. The poses are often passive. This means that the practitioner can hold them without straining their muscles. Yin yoga classes are usually longer than other styles of yoga. Yin teachers typically encourage students to hold individual poses for five minutes or even longer.

I'M NOT FLEXIBLE ENOUGH!

You don't need to be flexible to do yoga. Sure, some people can twist themselves into pretzels in yoga, but they are not very common. Most people who do yoga are working to improve their flexibility, as well as their strength.

Breath Control

Trying out yoga poses can mean stretching and bending your body all over the place. But another important part of yoga is learning to focus on and control your breath. These exercises will help you do so. Are you ready to practice breathing?

YOGA AND BREATHING

Controlled breathing, often called pranayama, is an important part of many styles of yoga. Learning to focus on your breath can help you calm down when feeling frightened or anxious. It can help you fall asleep more easily. And it can even help you cool down when you are hot!

Much of the pranayama in yoga simply involves linking breaths to movements. For example, a teacher might ask you to inhale as you stand up and exhale as you bend forward. Other times you might be asked to hold a pose for several breaths. Some pranayama activities are practiced in seated or reclining positions.

UJJAYI

One of the most common breathing exercises in yoga is called "ujjayi" (pronounced ooh-jai-ee). This gentle, smooth breath sounds similar to an ocean wave. Start by inhaling deeply. As you exhale, open your mouth wide and breathe as if you were trying to fog up a mirror. Halfway through your exhale, close your mouth and let the air from your lungs come out your nose. Continue to breathe in this way, making a soft hissing noise with both your inhales and exhales.

If these breath control exercises make you feel light-headed or dizzy, stop! Sit or lie down until you feel better. Never do breath work that makes you feel woozy.

Extended Exhales

This activity can help you calm down when you're stressed or anxious.
It can also help you fall asleep at night.

1 Lie on your back with one hand on your belly and breathe comfortably. Feel the way your belly rises and lowers with each breath.

2 Start to count the number of seconds each of your inhales takes. Then count the number of seconds each of your exhales takes. Do this for a few breaths.

3 Slowly, start to increase the number of seconds your exhales take. If your exhale takes 4 seconds, try to increase it to 5 seconds, then 6. Continue doing this until your exhale is twice as long as your inhale.

4 Repeat several times.

Cooling Breath

Feeling overheated? Try this breathing exercise to cool down quickly.

1 Sit in a comfortable position. Stick your tongue out and curl it, as though it were a straw.

2 Slightly lift your chin and inhale through your straw-shaped tongue.

3 Pull your tongue back into your mouth and exhale through your nose as you gently lower your chin.

4 Repeat several times.

Mindfulness and Meditation

Has anyone ever told you to "stop and smell the roses" or "live in the moment?" Have you ever heard someone talking about how they want to "be present?" If you go to yoga classes regularly, these pieces of advice might sound familiar. They are all related to one of the key components of yoga: mindfulness.

LEARNING TO BE MINDFUL

Mindfulness refers to a way of thinking that is encouraged in yoga. When people are mindful, they are focused on what they are doing at each moment. Mindfulness means paying special attention to each task.

PUT DOWN THAT PHONE!

If you have a cell phone, it might be standing between you and your mindfulness. It is so easy to check your phone while you're riding on the bus or watching TV. But this simple action is also a mega distraction. By looking at your phone, you're allowing your mind to focus on more than one thing at a time. Try to set a goal of only checking your phone once an hour. Then notice if this changes your ability to focus on what you're doing.

When you are mindful, you don't allow your mind to wander or become distracted. In yoga, mindful thinking often means concentrating on your breath and alignment in a pose.

Outside of yoga, mindfulness means not allowing yourself to get distracted by life's stresses. It involves devoting all of your focus to each activity or task you do. For example, if you are eating lunch, try to do so mindfully. Think about the texture, taste, and smell of your food instead of what TV show you want to watch next or what you'll wear to school tomorrow.

Boost your mood

Thinking mindfully is very beneficial. It can help improve your focus, boost your scores at school, and even help reduce stress and boost your mood. People who practice mindfulness are less easily distracted and have improved memories.

TIPS FOR THINKING MINDFULLY

1 Do one task at a time. Multi-tasking makes thinking mindfully almost impossible!

2 Slow down. Rushing through a task makes it hard to focus on what you are doing.

3 Turn inward. If you're feeling a bit overwhelmed, focus on a physical sensation, such as the way your belly moves when you breathe. This can help you concentrate on what is happening in the moment.

THINK CLEARLY!

ENJOY THE MOMENT

READY? SET? MEDITATE!

If you thought doing Bow Pose was hard, get ready for the real challenge: meditation. This quiet and still activity looks simple, but it can be very difficult.

Most people use the word "meditate" to mean focus, or think hard about something. In yoga, it often means something slightly different. In some practices, yoga meditation is the practice of resting the mind, or allowing it to be free of thought. This means resisting the urge to think about your homework or the school dance or the book you want to read. It means thinking about nothing—at all!

BE PATIENT!

Maybe you'll immediately be able to free your mind of all thoughts on your first try. But most people have to work at meditation for months, years, and even decades. Be patient with yourself. The process of learning to meditate is just as good for you as meditation itself.

CLEAR YOUR MIND

RECHARGE

READY TO GIVE IT A SHOT?

1 Set the scene: Find a quiet place where you can be alone. Turn down the lights and turn off any music, television, or electronics that might distract you.

2 Sit comfortably. Some people choose to sit with their legs crossed on the ground. If that is not comfortable for you, try sitting on the ground with your legs extended, or in a chair. You won't be able to meditate if you are distracted by discomfort!

3 Close your eyes and turn your attention to your breath. Pay attention to the way your breath sounds and feels.

4 Eventually, allow your mind to release all thoughts, even those that are related to your breathing.

Begin your meditation practice by sitting once a day for just a few minutes at a time. Start out at three minutes. Then, as you get more comfortable, slowly start to add minutes. Use the timer on your phone so that you are not distracted by looking at a clock.

It's Yoga Practice, Not Yoga Perfect

As you begin your yoga journey, be patient. Some activities will be easy for you, and others will be difficult. You might be surprised to find that you are a natural at meditation, but that breath control drives you nuts. This is all okay. Doing yoga is about challenging yourself to grow and learn, while being gentle and kind.

Yoga for Life

You may have come to the end of the book, but your yoga journey is just beginning. Yoga is a lifelong activity. People do it well into their eighties, nineties, and beyond, because it can be adapted to all ability levels. Some days, you might want to practice some very difficult asanas and work up a sweat. Other days, you might choose to simply sit quietly and stretch for a few minutes. Yoga is simply a way to feel good, mentally, physically, and emotionally. If you can keep this in mind, you'll find that your yoga practice feels perfect, no matter what it looks like.

Useful Links

Check out this website to learn all about yoga:
kidshealth.org/teen/food_fitness/
    exercise/yoga.html

Try this site out to watch videos of yoga poses, sequences, breathing exercises, and meditation:
www.doyogawithme.com/yoga_classes

Head to this website to learn more about the history of yoga, yoga philosophies, correct alignment in different yoga poses, and more:
yogajournal.com

Learn more about some of the philosophies behind yoga at this website:
www.britannica.com/topic/
    Yoga-philosophy

Type words into this translator to learn the Sanskrit version, including the Devanagari script:
www.spokensanskrit.de

*Website information is correct at time of going to press. The publishers cannot accept liability for any information or links found on third-party websites.

This site shows you how to pronounce the names of some of the most common asanas:
yogainternational.com/brochure/
    sanskrit-pronunciation-guide

If you're in the mood for simplicity, try following along with these basic yoga sequences.
www.dummies.com/how-to/content/
    yoga-routines-for-teens.html

Podcasts are a great way to enjoy yoga at home. Try one of YogaDownload's 20-minute sessions.
itunes.apple.com/us/podcast/20-min.-
    yoga-sessions-from/id259744514/

Glossary

alignment the correct positioning of your body parts in a yoga pose. Practicing with good alignment reduces the chances of becoming injured.

asana yoga pose

asymmetrical pose yoga pose in which both sides of the body are not equal. For example, a twisting pose is asymmetrical.

Buddhism religious tradition and philosophy that comes from ancient India

cardiovascular type of exercise that challenges the heart and lungs

controlled breathing breath that is purposefully regulated by briefly holding the breath, elongating the breath, or changing the rhythm of the breath.

core the muscles of your stomach, back, chest, and pelvis

elongate to lengthen or stretch

endorphins type of hormone, or chemical, secreted by the brain that makes people feel good

engage to activate, flex, or tighten

exhale to breathe out

guru teacher

Hinduism religious tradition that comes from Ancient India

inhale to breathe in

meditate to free the mind of all thought

mindfulness a way of thinking that encourages focus

mudra a symbolic hand gesture

passive without resistance. Passive yoga poses typically do not involve much muscular challenge.

philosophy a set of views or beliefs about life

pose way of holding the body

pranayama breathing exercises practiced as part of yoga

rejuvenate to refresh, restore, or energize

restorative restful or healing

Sanskrit an ancient language from India. Sanskrit is written left to right in a script that is called Devanagari.

spine another word for the backbone, made up of the bones that extend from the skull down through the tailbone

stress emotional tension that results from different types of pressures

yoga strap long, strong strap made of canvas, cotton, or other materials that can be used to modify different yoga poses

Index